WORD
SPELLING

BOOK FOUR
Ronald Ridout

Ginn is an imprint of Pearson Education Limited, a company incorporated in England and Wales, having its registered office at Edinburgh Gate, Harlow, Essex, CM20 2JE. Registered company number: 872828

www.pearsonglobalschools.com

Text © Ronald Ridout, 1957

First published 1957
Revised edition 2008
Reprinted in 2015

20 19 18 17 16 15
IMP: 20 19 18 17 16 15

British Library Cataloguing in Publication Data is available from the British Library on request.

ISBN 978 0 435996 94 9

Typeset and illustrated by Planman Technologies India Pvt. Ltd
Original illustrations © Pearson Education Ltd, 2008
Cover design by Tony Richardson
Cover illustration © Pearson Education Ltd, 2008
Printed and bound in India by Gopsons Papers Ltd

Every effort has been made to contact copyright holders of material reproduced in this book. Any omissions will be rectified in subsequent printings if notice is given to the publishers.

PREFACE

In Book Four of *Word Perfect Spelling* we have reached a stage in the child's development when the mastery of spelling rules may reasonably be expected to help in forming correct spelling habits. All the simpler rules have, therefore, been included, though much of the work still achieves its object less formally.

As with the earlier books, words and patterns are kept in constant revision, while new patterns, subjects and rules are introduced at a steady rate. Ample scope is also provided for prepared dictation, the importance of which at this stage is increasing. But, since it avails little to be able to spell a word if its meaning is unknown, as the words become more difficult, greater emphasis is now placed upon the understanding of their meaning and usage.

The Introductory and eight main books of *Word Perfect Spelling* provide a systematic course in spelling and vocabulary from the ages of 6 or 7 to 15+. Though in the first place it is correct spelling that they aim at, the books will at the same time help the pupil to gain complete mastery over the fundamental vocabulary needed by him or her at the various stages of his or her career.

Placing words in certain patterns enables them to be recalled with a greater ease, both in the short and long term. In addition, it allows one key word to unlock many more. This is the main method used in this series, although other styles have been used for specific exercises.

The course, however, does not end with the listing of words: it only begins there. The words have to be linked with the child's interests and brought to life by challenging activities. These activities are in themselves valuable aids to the teaching of English, but they have a vital function in improving spelling.

table	lawn	pilot	paper
chairs	roses	airliner	stories
carpet	lilies	engine	teacher
people	daisies	runway	children
eight	cheese	monkey	bread
twelve	matches	lion	potatoes
twenty	biscuits	tiger	carrots
hundred	toothpaste	elephant	pudding
beak	words	Sunday	toffees
claws	sentences	Monday	chocolates
eyes	questions	Tuesday	packets
feathers	answers	Wednesday	money

These are words that you have met before. Can you still spell them?
Write the group of four most likely to be found:

1 in a garden
2 in an English book
3 on a calendar
4 at a sweet shop
5 at the grocer's
6 at an airport
7 in a living-room
8 at the zoo
9 in an Arithmetic book
10 in a classroom
11 on a bird
12 on the dinner table

Use a dictionary to check your spelling as you make your own lists
of four things you might find:

13 in your bedroom
14 at the seaside
15 at the station
16 on a farm

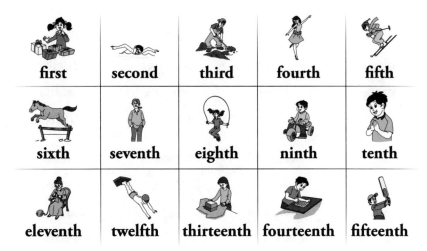

| first | second | third | fourth | fifth |
| eleventh | twelfth | thirteenth | fourteenth | fifteenth |

Mrs Jones knitting
Helen dancing
Simon swimming
Mr Parker digging
a pony jumping
a girl skipping
John batting

Andrew diving
Keith skiing on the snow
Margaret wrapping a parcel
George clapping the winner
Sheila choosing a present
a toddler cycling
Richard writing a letter

old Mr Williams smoking his pipe

Using the above phrases, write a sentence about each picture, beginning like this:

1 The first picture shows Sheila choosing a present.

dancing	swimming	jumping	Sheila
diving	skipping	wrapping	Keith
skiing	knitting	choosing	Margaret
writing	clapping	cycling	George

beard	ground	earth	depart
peach	bough	heard	report
heath	thousand	search	Robert
easiest	should	earnest	pretend

high	field	truth	church
brightest	shield	board	though
word	health	laugh	heart
world	heaviest	friend	fetch

Can you still spell these familiar words? Write them in eight groups of four according to whether they end in:

1 th **2** nd **3** ch **4** rd **5** ld **6** st **7** rt **8** gh

Write the words from the list that rhyme with:

9 teach **10** sigh **11** Ruth **12** stealth **13** low

Next write the words from the list that are opposites of:

14 hardest **15** dullest **16** low **17** arrive **18** lies

Now write the words that mean the same as:

19 moor **20** tall **21** chum **22** leave **23** hunt

24 Instead of *f* in <u>fetch</u> write: *sk, str, wr*.
25 Instead of *p* in <u>peach</u> write: *b, r, t, pr*.
26 Instead of *th* in <u>heath</u> write: *l, p, r, t, ve, ter*.
27 Instead of *sh* in <u>should</u> write: *c, w*.
28 Instead of *w* in <u>weather</u> write: *f, h, l*.

aunt	father	grandfather	cousin
uncle	mother	grandmother	babies
nephew	brother	husband	parents
niece	sister	wife	children

Complete each sentence with the right word from the box.

1 Peter's mother and father are his _____.
2 The wife of Mary's father is Mary's _____.
3 The husband of Mary's mother is Mary's _____.
4 Children under two years are usually called _____.
5 The father of my father is my _____.
6 The mother of my father is my _____.
7 My mother's sister is my _____.
8 My mother's brother is my _____.
9 The son of my aunt is my _____.
10 Margaret is her uncle's _____, and Roger is his uncle's _____.
11 John's father is the _____ of John's mother.
12 John's mother is the _____ of John's father.
13 Robert is Susan's _____, and Susan is Robert's _____, because they both have the same parents.
14 The plural of child is _____.
15 Write the words in the box in alphabetical order. Remember that if two words begin with the same letter, you must look at the second letter. Thus **children** comes before **cousin**, because **h** comes before **o**. (Note: **grandfather** comes before **grandmother**.)

The first place that I can remember at all well was a large pleasant meadow with a pond of clear water in it. Some shady trees leaned over it, and rushes and water lilies grew at the deep end. On one side we looked over a hedge at a ploughed field. On the other side we looked over a gate at our master's house. (From *Black Beauty* by Anna Sewell.)

field	**pleasant**	**edge**	**plough**
belief	**meadow**	**hedge**	**bough**
believe	**measure**	**bridge**	**water**
piece	**pleasure**	**judge**	**remember**

1 Instead of *f* in <u>field</u> write: *sh, y*.
2 Instead of *ve* in <u>believe</u> write: *f, ver, ving, ved*.
3 In front of <u>dge</u> write: *e, he, we, le, ju, bu, ba, do*.
4 Instead of *m* in <u>measure</u> write: *pl, tr*.
5 Write <u>remember</u> without the prefix **re-**.
6 Instead of *p* in <u>piece</u> write: *n*.
7 Write the singular (one only) of: **lilies, cities, pennies**.

Cut them on Monday, you cut them for health;
Cut them on Tuesday, you cut them for wealth;
Cut them on Wednesday, you cut them for news;
Cut them on Thursday, a new pair of shoes;
Cut them on Friday, you cut them for sorrow;
Cut them on Saturday, see your true love tomorrow;
Cut them on Sunday, ill luck be with you all the week.

Monday	Friday	wealth	sorrow
Tuesday	Saturday	wealthy	borrow
Wednesday	Sunday	healthy	tomorrow
Thursday	untrue	unhealthy	narrow

One way of making the opposite of a word is to put the prefix **un-** in front of it. This means not. Thus **untrue** means not true, and is the opposite of **true**. Similarly **unhealthy** is the opposite of **healthy** and **unsafe** is the opposite of **safe**.

By using the prefix **un-** make the opposites of these words:

1 true	**5** dressed	**9** even	**13** healthy	**17** sound
2 wise	**6** closed	**10** level	**14** pleasant	**18** seen
3 kind	**7** covered	**11** alike	**15** happy	**19** afraid
4 clean	**8** tied	**12** known	**16** common	**20** eaten

love	loving	lovely	bravery
hope	hoping	hopeful	peaceful
brave	braver	bravely	ripeness
taste	tasty	tasteless	paddler
meddle	meddling	meddlesome	famous

When you add a suffix to a word ending in a single e, you must drop the **e** if the suffix begins with a vowel (a, e, i, o, u). Example: *use —using—used*.

But if the suffix begins with a consonant (any other letter), you must keep the **e**.
Example: *use—useful—useless*.

Notice that if the suffix is y, it counts as a vowel.
Example: *stone —stony; taste—tasty*.

Make new words by adding *-ing* to these verbs:

1 taste **2** waste **3** have **4** live **5** stare **6** glance

Make adverbs by adding *-ly* to these adjectives:

7 safe **8** nice **9** false **10** square **11** wise **12** purpose

Make nouns by adding the suffix *-er* to these verbs:

13 love **14** move **15** waste **16** make **17** bake **18** tease

Make adjectives by adding *-y* to these nouns:

19 taste **20** haste **21** breeze **22** chance **23** craze **24** bone

Make adjectives by adding *-ful* to these nouns:

25 peace **26** care **27** use **28** grace **29** waste **30** spite

Make new words by adding *-ous*, *-less* or *-able* to these:

31 hope **32** fame **33** nerve **34** move **35** care **36** love

Maureen my sister and I fell out,
And what do you think it was all about?
She loved coffee and I loved tea,
And that was the reason we couldn't agree.

agree	couldn't	reason	lovable
coffee	wouldn't	season	agreeable
referee	didn't	reasonable	beautiful
Maureen	won't	unbeatable	treason

Read the rule on page 9, and then make adjectives by adding *-able* to these verbs:

1 reason	3 agree	5 love	7 use	9 desire
2 remark	4 disagree	6 like	8 cure	10 obtain

The apostrophe (') may mean that a letter has been left out, or perhaps several letters have been left out. Thus **couldn't** stands for **could not** and **I'd** for **I would**. Now pair each of these with its full meaning:

11 it's	who is	19 don't	shall not
12 here's	there will	20 won't	it was
13 who's	I am	21 shan't	I would
14 they're	we are	22 hasn't	would not
15 there'll	you have	23 wouldn't	do not
16 you've	it is	24 you'd	has not
17 I'm	they are	25 I'd	you had
18 we're	here is	26 'twas	will not

Our master was a good, kind man. He gave us good food, good lodging and kind words. He spoke as kindly to us as he did to his little children. We were all fond of him, and my mother loved him dearly. When she saw him by the gate, she would neigh and trot joyfully up to him. (From *Black Beauty* by Anna Sewell.)

joyful	merry	colour	neigh
joyfully	merrily	favour	weigh
tidy	easy	favourite	lodging
tidily	easily	favourable	flavour

Notice that to add *-ly* to a word ending in **y**, you must first change the **y** into **i** and then add *-ly*. Now make adverbs by adding *-ly* to these adjectives:

1 easy	4 nasty	7 joyful	10 weary
2 sudden	5 steady	8 busy	11 greedy
3 merry	6 noisy	9 careful	12 beautiful

January	first	July	seventh
February	second	August	eighth
March	third	September	ninth
April	fourth	October	tenth
May	fifth	November	eleventh
June	sixth	December	twelfth

Write twelve sentences, beginning like this:

1 January is the first month.
2 February is the second month.

Thirty days hath September,
April, June and November.
All the rest have thirty-one,
Excepting February alone,
And that has twenty-eight days clear
And twenty-nine in each leap year.

Write these sentences, putting in the missing words:

13 _____ usually has twenty-eight days.
14 Every fourth year February has _____ days.
15 August always has _____ days.
16 _____ is the first and _____ is the last month of the year.
17 The month between July and September is _____.
18 The four months ending in y are _____, _____, _____ and _____.
19 April, _____, _____ and _____ all have thirty days.
20 January, _____, _____, _____, _____, _____ and _____ have thirty-one days.

door	window	dwelling	hedge
path	chimney	gutter	garden
roof	drain	passage	kitchen
porch	building	garage	entrance

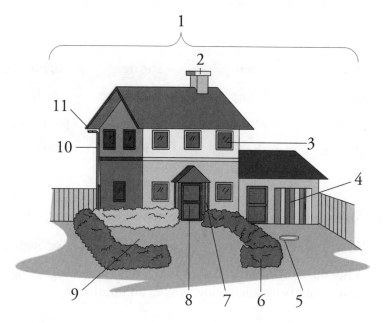

Write the numbers 1–11 and put the right name beside each.

12 Instead of *d* in <u>door</u> write: *p, fl, m.*

13 Instead of *dw* in <u>dwelling</u> write: *t, sp, sw.*

14 Instead of *p* in <u>porch</u> write: *t, sc.*

15 Instead of *g* in <u>gutter</u> write: *b, c, m, sh, fl, st, spl.*

16 Instead of *gar* in <u>garage</u> write: *w, st, pass, post, sav, saus, dam, man, mess, voy, band, pack, cour, cott.*

Good King Wenceslas looked out
On the Feast of Stephen,
When the snow lay round about
Deep and crisp and even.
Brightly shone the moon that night,
Though the frost was cruel,
When a poor man came in sight,
Gathering winter fuel.

fuel	**even**	**shone**	**turkey**
cruel	**event**	**chicken**	**holly**
cruet	**evening**	**berries**	**pudding**
Stephen	**gathering**	**Christmas**	**stuffing**

Write the words from the carol that rhyme with:

1 beast   **2** lisp   **3** lost   **4** night   **5** fuel   **6** Stephen

7 Write the names of the seasons in the right order, beginning with spring (summer, spring, winter, autumn).

Arrange each of these lists in alphabetical order:

8	**9**	**10**	**11**
dinner	feast	Stephen	crackers
supper	crisp	Christopher	jellies
stuffing	carol	Catherine	berries
breakfast	even	George	evenings
puddings	gather	Gordon	turkeys
seasoning	frosty	Philip	geese
goose	fuel	Percy	children

1 **b** ☐☐☐☐☐ This goes across a river.   (page 7)

2 ☐☐ **s** ☐ **e** ☐☐☐☐ Without any taste.   (9)

3 ☐☐☐ **r** **u** ☐☐☐ The second month of the year.   (12)

4 ☐☐☐ **p** **h** ☐☐☐ Largest land animal in the world.   (3)

5 ☐☐☐☐ **e** ☐ The plural of baby.   (6)

6 ☐☐☐☐ **v** ☐ A dozen.   (3)

7 ☐ **w** ☐☐☐☐☐☐ Moving through the water.   (4)

8 ☐☐☐☐☐ **t** ☐ Next after the seventh.   (12)

9 ☐☐ **c** **I** ☐☐☐ Moving feet on pedals.   (4)

10 ☐☐ **i** **e** ☐☐ The opposite of enemy.   (5)

11 ☐☐ **u** ☐☐ The opposite of kind.   (14)

12 ☐☐ **e** ☐☐ A girl is this to her uncle.   (6)

13 ☐ **e** ☐☐☐☐☐☐ The opposite of to forget.   (7)

14 ☐☐☐ **o** ☐☐ Very well known.   (9)

15 ☐ **e** ☐☐☐☐☐ The opposite of poor.   (8)

16 ☐☐ **r** ☐☐☐ House for a car.   (13)

17 ☐ **o** ☐☐☐☐☐ The day after today.   (8)

18 ☐ **n** ☐☐☐☐☐☐☐ Not able to be beaten.   (10)

19 ☐☐☐☐☐☐ The cry of a horse.   (11)

20 ☐☐☐☐☐☐☐☐☐ Possessing beauty.   (10)

21 ☐☐☐☐☐☐☐☐☐ The day between Tuesday and Thursday.   (8)

22 ☐☐☐☐☐ The opposite of to arrive.   (5)

23 ☐☐☐☐☐☐ This is used to turn over soil.   (7)

24 ☐☐☐☐☐ More brave.   (9)

25 ☐☐☐☐☐☐☐ Judge of play in a game.   (10)

26 ☐☐☐☐☐☐☐☐ The one liked better than the others.   (11)

able	listen	Peter	pitch
table	hasten	Mary	stretch
capable	often	Michael	catch
lovable	dozen	Margaret	scratch

(1)

stare	salt	ticket	sugar
spare	alter	bucket	potatoes
share	chalk	size	chocolates
daring	stalk	prize	biscuits

(2)

fleet	skipping	niece	rule
queer	paddling	piece	ruler
greedy	knitting	shield	loser
freedom	wrapping	believe	lover

(3)

For dictation

The story called "Black Beauty" was written about a hundred and thirty years ago. Anna Sewell wrote it because she was fond of horses. She pretended that the horse was telling his own story. In this way she tried to make people understand horses better. She hoped that they would then look after them well and never be cruel to them. It became very famous and is still read by thousands of children every year.

dislike	repeat	delay	expand
disgrace	remain	depend	express
discuss	refuse	demand	expense
disgust	reserve	deliver	excite

Make new words by putting *re-* in front of these:

1 new   **2** mind   **3** pair   **4** mark   **5** move   **6** cover

Make new words by putting the prefix *ex-* in front of these:

7 change   **8** claim   **9** it   **10** plain   **11** port

Make new words by adding the prefix *dis-* to these:

12 grace   **13** cover   **14** like   **15** please   **16** miss

Make new words by adding the prefix *re-* to these:

17 turn   **18** ward   **19** tire   **20** quest   **21** verse

Make new words by adding the prefix *be-* to these:

22 come   **23** long   **24** low   **25** side   **26** ware

There are two syllables in **refuse** (re-fuse). Show the two syllables in each of these words:

27 express   **29** exact   **31** review   **33** behave
28 discuss   **30** demand   **32** betray   **34** exchange

There are three syllables in **disorder** (dis-or-der). Show the three syllables in each of these words:

35 reorder   **37** disgusting   **39** deliver   **41** exciting
36 discover   **38** disgraceful   **40** repeated   **42** expensive

Make new words using one of these: *re-, ex-, dis-, de-*.

43 part   **44** tent   **45** able   **46** late   **47** trust   **48** serve

inform	confuse	excuse	platform
intend	conduct	except	perform
inquire	content	permit	giant
interest	concert	admit	servant

Make the words asked for from the syllables in the boxes:

| mit   ad   per |

1 to allow
2 to let in

| form   per   in |

3 to act in public
4 to supply with facts

| ant   gi   serv |

5 huge imaginary man
6 person employed by another

| con   fuse   cert |

7 musical entertainment
8 to mix up or bewilder

| cuse   ex   cept |

9 a reason or explanation for
10 leaving out

| duct   tent   con |

11 satisfied
12 to lead or guide

Confusing is made up of three syllables (con-fus-ing). Split each of these into three syllables:

13 conducting   17 pretended   21 interest
14 performing   18 conducted   22 excuses
15 excusing   19 disgraceful   23 conductor
16 contented   20 repeated   24 inquiry

Sometimes a rough boy called Dick would come into our field to pick blackberries. When he had eaten all he wanted, he would have what he called fun with the colts. He threw sticks and stones at them to make

them gallop. We did not mind very much because we could gallop away. But sometimes a stone would hit us and hurt us.

One morning he played this game and did not know that the master was in the next field watching. He scrambled over the hedge and caught Dick in the act.

"You are a naughty boy to chase the colts," he grumbled. "That will be quite enough. I never want to see you on my farm again." (From *Black Beauty* by Anna Sewell.)

caught	gallop	rough	scramble
taught	carrot	enough	grumble
naughty	ribbon	tough	bundle
daughter	cotton	morning	bangle

1 Instead of *b* in <u>bangle</u> write: *d, m, t*.
2 Instead of *gr* in <u>grumble</u> write: *h, m, t, j, f, r, st*.
3 Instead of *co* in <u>cotton</u> write: *mu, bu, glu*.
4 Instead of *c* in <u>carrot</u> write: *p*.
5 Instead of *scr* in <u>scramble</u> write: *g, r, br*.
6 Instead of *op* in <u>gallop</u> write: *ant, ey, on, ows*.

sailor	major	senior	size
tailor	motor	junior	gaze
actor	doctor	visitor	gazing
tractor	author	monitor	razor

To complete these sentences correctly, use each word from the box once only.

1 An _____ performs on the stage.
2 A person who writes books is called an _____.
3 A _____ makes clothes.
3 Major Senior uses a _____ to shave off his beard.
5 Robert takes _____ three in shoes.
6 The _____ in my class looks after the library books.
7 The farmer uses a _____ to pull his plough.
8 The _____ in charge of a ship is called the captain.
9 The word _____ means the opposite of minor, but it may also mean an army officer.
10 _____ rhymes with craze and means to look hard.
11 A _____ school takes pupils from 7 to 11.
12 _____ pupils, aged 11 upwards, go to secondary schools.
13 Anyone who calls to see you at your house is a _____.
14 When Mr Lazy grew too fat he had to go to see a _____.
15 Any engine used to drive a machine is called a _____.
16 Having finished, he sat _____ at his beautiful work.

ankle	forehead
ear	finger
elbow	wrist
thigh	eyebrow
calf	mouth
palm	shoulder
knee	stomach
thumb	nose

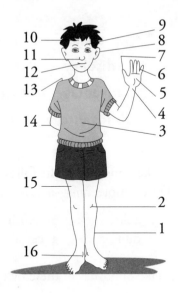

Write the names in the same order as the numbers (1–16).

Write the words that rhyme with:

17 south	**19** twist	**21** boulder	**23** toes
18 half	**20** calm	**22** sigh	**24** come

Write the adjectives from which these adverbs have been formed. Example: *merrily is formed from merry.*

25 merrily	**27** hungrily	**29** ably	**31** beautifully
26 angrily	**28** wearily	**30** gently	**32** capably

Write the adverbs that can be formed from these adjectives:

33 happy	**35** careful	**37** simple	**39** horrible
34 hasty	**36** hopeful	**38** feeble	**40** reliable

obey	expect	Britain	discover
disobey	respect	certain	contain
advantage	disrespect	fountain	damaged
disadvantage	respectful	mountain	protect

Make opposites of the following by using the prefix **un-**.
For example: *safe—unsafe, tied—untied*.

1 able   3 selfish   5 cover   7 expected
2 done   4 certain   6 damaged   8 protected

Make opposites of these by using the prefix **dis-**.

9 obey   12 grace   15 agree   18 cover
10 trust   13 like   16 pleased   19 advantage
11 mount   14 appear   17 respect   20 respectful

Break into syllables each word in the box, beginning like this:

21 o-bey   22 dis-o-bey.

There are ten with two syllables, five with three, and one with four.

37 Instead of *cer* in certain write: *cur, con, s, cap, ob*.
38 Instead of *dam* in damage write: *sav, voy, man, pass*.

Notice these: *waste—wasteful—wastefully*. Make a similar series from each of these:

39 care   41 faith   43 cheer   45 beauty   47 disgrace
40 truth   42 joy   44 use   46 mercy   48 plenty

I shall never forget the first train that ran by. I was feeding quietly near the fence that separates the field from the railway, when I heard a strange sound in the distance. With a rush and a clatter, a long black thing flew past, and was gone almost before I could draw my breath. I turned and galloped to the other side of the field. During the day many more trains went by. Some drew up at the station close by, making an awful shriek before they stopped. At first I thought they were dreadful. But as these terrible monsters never came into the field or did me any harm, I soon began to ignore them. (Adapted from *Black Beauty* by Anna Sewell.)

nation	breath	strange	monster
station	awful	stranger	shriek
motion	clatter	danger	separate
mention	terrible	distance	ignore

Fill the gaps with the right words from the box.

1 When you draw your ____ you take air into your lungs.
2 A ____ is a place where trains stop.
3 To ____ something is to take no notice of it.
4 A ____ is a huge thing that frightens you.
5 A loud sharp noise is called a ____.
6 To ____ means to keep apart.

novel	manage	porter	carpenter
novelist	manager	grocer	passenger
cycle	travel	artist	explorer
cyclist	traveller	typist	bricklayer

1 **Cyclist, typist, explorer, manager** are formed from: **cycle, type, explore, manage.** Write out the rule from page 9 that tells you how to form such words.

2 Notice that **travel** doubles the **l** before adding **-er**. In the same way **forget** doubles the t before adding a suffix beginning with a vowel (*forgetting, forgotten*), but not before a suffix beginning with a consonant (*forgetful*). Now add **-er** to these:
(*a*) travel   (*b*) jewel   (*c*) begin   (*d*) forget

3 Add **-ing** to the following:
(*a*) forget   (*b*) begin   (*c*) travel   (*d*) level   (*e*) control

Choose the right words from the box to complete these:

4 A person who rides a cycle is called a ____.
5 Novels are long story books and are written by the ____.
6 The ____ makes and repairs things in wood.
7 Amundsen was the ____ who first reached the South Pole.
8 A ____ writes letters on a typewriter.
9 The person who sits by the driver is his ____.
10 A ____ is a person who is in charge of a shop or office.

knife	wrap	weigh	thumb
knuckle	wrist	weight	crumb
knead	whole	eighty	doubt
knowledge	sword	height	debt

1 Which is the silent letter or letters in each group above?
2 Rewrite the following in four groups in the same way:

frighten	climbed	wrapping	wholly
written	fought	eighth	knock
knives	although	doubter	bomber
knotted	knitting	combing	wreck

How would you arrange the first list in the box in alphabetical order? If the first two letters of any two words are the same, we must look at the third letters. Thus **knead** will come before **knife**, because **e** comes before **i**. Similarly **knife** will come before **knowledge** because **i** comes before **o**. And so on. Now arrange the following in alphabetical order:

3 the first list in the box
4 the second list in the box
5 all the words beginning with **w** in both boxes
6 knob, knit, knead, knuckle, knack
7 whom, wrapper, wringer, wreckage, white, whole
8 dumb, debt, delight, deaf, demand, doubt, deny, depart

islands	loaves	factories	potatoes
yachts	thieves	difficulties	tomatoes
churches	chiefs	libraries	pianos
stitches	dwarfs	railways	geese

Remember that singular means one only, and plural means more than one. Remember also that **a, e, i, o, u** are vowels and all the other letters of the alphabet are consonants.

Rules for forming the plural

1 The usual way to form the plural of a noun is to add *-s* to the singular.
   Example: *carpet—carpets, island—islands.*
2 But nouns ending in a hissing sound (s, sh, ch, x, z) add *-es*.
   Example: *dress—dresses, church—churches.*
3 Some ending in f change the f to v and then add *-es*.
   Example: *loaf—loaves, shelf—shelves.*
4 A few ending in **f** simply add *-s*.
   Example: *roofs, cliffs, chiefs.*
5 If the noun ends in **y** with a consonant before it, you must change the **y** into **i** and then add *-es*.
   Example: *lady—ladies, factory—factories.*
6 But if the noun ends in **y** with a vowel before it, you simply add *-s*.
   Example: *valley—valleys, railway—railways.*
7 Some ending in **o** add *-es*.
   Example: *potatoes, mottoes.*
8 Others ending in **o** simply add *-s*.
   Example: *pianos, ponchos.*
9 Some are irregular.
   Example: *mouse—mice, woman—women.*

heroes	crows	solos	hoofs	monkeys
mangoes	swallows	pianos	cliffs	chimneys
cargoes	sparrows	banjos	gulfs	valleys
firemen	babies	witches	wives	—
children	injuries	glasses	leaves	—
teeth	pennies	wishes	halves	—

Each group has formed its plural according to one of the rules on page 24. Write the groups in the same order as the rules, numbering them, like the rules, 1–9.

Number 10 has formed its plural according to rule 1; number 11 according to rule 2, and so on. Write out the singular forms:

10 robins	**13** scarfs	**16** volcanoes
11 atlases	**14** daisies	**17** ponchos
12 knives	**15** runways	**18** women

The ways in which these nouns form their plurals are also in the same order as the rules. Write out their plural forms:

19 object	**22** cuff	**25** potato
20 branch	**23** cherry	**26** solo
21 thief	**24** chimney	**27** foot

Rewrite these, changing the italicised nouns to singular:

28 The *thieves* stole *dresses*, *watches*, *knives* and *pianos*.
29 These *firemen* are *heroes* in those *cities*.
30 The *children* were picking cherries in the *valleys*.
31 These *shelves* hold *novels*, *atlases* and *plays*.

midnight	although	warmth	shepherd
delightful	altogether	wardrobe	popular
frightful	welcome	warning	regular
already	fulfil	quarter	particular

A red sky at night
Is the shepherd's delight.
A red sky in the morning
Is the shepherd's warning.

The south wind brings wet weather,
The north wind wet and cold together.
The west wind always brings us rain;
The east wind blows it back again.

Here is an extra list of words. They are all common ones that you will need to be able to spell; but they are rather odd, and each one needs learning separately.

vase	laughter	owe	several
iron	comfort	due	worship
apron	poetry	else	ocean
union	diary	ache	wander

1 ` | | | o | r ` A person who writes books.   (page 20)

2 ` e | x | | | | ` To grow bigger.   (17)

3 ` | y | | | | | ` Anyone who rides a cycle.   (24)

4 ` | | | | s | s ` To talk over.   (17)

5 ` | | | a | | ` To say again.   (17)

6 ` | | | k | ` A loud sharp noise.   (23)

7 ` | | | i | | | ` A stopping place for trains.   (23)

8 ` | | c | | | | ` A musical entertainment.   (18)

9 ` | | v | | | ` Any person employed by another.   (18)

10 ` | | a | | ` To mix by pressing and squeezing.   (25)

11 ` | | | o | | ` To run fast like a horse.   (19)

12 ` | | g | | ` The opposite of tender.   (19)

13 ` | | | r | ` The opposite of minor.   (20)

14 ` | z | | ` Sharp tool to shave with.   (20)

15 ` | | | | | e | | ` The plural of library.   (26)

16 ` | | | t | | ` The part between hand and arm.   (21)

17 ` | | | | ` The inside of the hand.   (21)

18 ` | | | | | | | | ` The plural of injury.   (27)

19 ` | | | | | | ` The opposite of to obey.   (21)

20 ` | | | | | | ` The opposite of doubtful.   (22)

21 ` | | | | | | | | ` Showing that you look up to some-
one.   (22)

22 ` | | | | | | ` Person who uses a typewriter.   (24)

23 ` | | | | | | ` To keep apart.   (23)

24 ` | | | | | | ` To take no notice of.   (23)

25 ` | | | | ` Something owed to another.   (25)

26 ` | | | | | ` Lack of belief or sureness.   (25)

27 ` | | | | | ` Light sailing boats for racing.   (26)

children	nation	wrong	mountain
women	station	among	country
piece	question	across	France
shriek	dictation	avoid	advance

(1)

excuse	worry	extra	curtain
refuse	carry	except	certain
pure	carrot	excite	obtain
picture	barrow	explain	captain

(2)

Terrible	protect	disagree	people
horrible	respectful	disadvantage	beautiful
traveller	merciful	disgusting	shepherd
beginner	unhappily	disgraceful	chimney

(3)

For dictation

One night a terrible thing happened. The stable containing Black Beauty and several other horses caught on fire. The horses became very excited. They trembled all over. They were so frightened that they refused to leave the building. It seemed as if they would all be burned alive. Then James, the groom, fought his way through the smoke and flames. He tied his scarf over the eyes of Black Beauty, spoke to him gently and led him out into the yard.

square	bowl	burn	declare
beware	growth	furnish	Glasgow
compare	pillow	murder	purpose
prepare	follow	purple	surprise

1 Instead of *n* in <u>burn</u> write: *st, ner, ning, den, glar.*
2 Instead of *th* in <u>growth</u> write: *n, ing, er, l.*
3 Instead of *pi* in <u>pillow</u> write: *fo, ho, ye, fe, sha, swa.*
4 Instead of *pose* in <u>purpose</u> write: *ple, se, chase, sue.*
5 Instead of *prise* in <u>surprise</u> write: *name, round, mount.*
6 Instead of *fur* in <u>furnish</u> write: *fi, pu, var, Spa.*
7 Write the five words in the box that rhyme with dare.

Read the rule on page 7. Then add *-ing* and *-ed* to these:

8 prepare   10 murder   12 compare   14 surround
9 follow   11 surprise 13 furnish   15 glare

Pair each numbered word with its opposite.

16 follow   reckless
17 finish   deep
18 careful   lead
19 shallow   common
20 vanish   peace
21 rare   begin
22 warfare   sell
23 purchase appear

24 dwarfs   straight
25 curse   together
26 curly   bless
27 pursue   unready
28 separate lead
29 further   giants
30 prepared ignorance
31 knowledge nearer

stoop	labour	huge	journey
smooth	harbour	amuse	armour
loose	humour	future	kangaroo
choose	honour	introduce	usual

Write the words from the box that mean the opposite of:

1 tiny   **2** past   **3** rough   **4** firm   **5** dishonour

Now write the words that mean the same as:

6 work   **7** entertain   **8** vast   **9** voyage   **10** elect

11 Write the nine words from the box that can be made from this sentence, using each letter once only in any one word:

MANY YACHTS SAILED INTO THE HARBOUR

Write the plurals of these words:

12 harbour   **14** pillow   **16** injury   **18** kangaroo
13 journey   **15** goose   **17** diary   **19** guess

Pair each numbered word with its synonym (word of same meaning):

20 loose	judge	**28** often	rarely
21 huge	pursue	**29** seldom	burglars
22 choose	wobbly	**30** careless	frequently
23 referee	entertainment	**31** vanish	purchase
24 usual	gigantic	**32** buy	burden
25 follow	uncommon	**33** thieves	unusual
26 rare	ordinary	**34** strange	disappear
27 amusement	select	**35** weight	reckless

The Wright brothers were famous American airmen. In the beginning they made only gliders. Then one day they had the brilliant idea of fixing an engine to one of the gliders. The engine drove a propeller at the rear of the aeroplane.

When everything was ready, they took their machine to the top of a hill. The engine roared, and the machine gathered speed. At last it rose into the air and travelled a few hundred metres at fifty kilometres an hour. It was the first proper aeroplane in the world to fly.

travelled	**engine**	**proper**	**America**
propeller	**machine**	**property**	**American**
beginning	**divide**	**famous**	**Africa**
brilliant	**aeroplane**	**dangerous**	**African**

Fill the gaps with the right words from the box:

1 A _____ person is one who is very well known.
2 An _____ is a flying machine driven by an engine.
3 The engine drives a _____ that makes the aeroplane fly.
4 An _____ is a person from the United States of America.
5 An _____ is a person from Africa.
6 _____ means very bright or very clever.
7 The start means the same as the _____.
8 The things belonging to a person are called his _____.

towel	tempt	silent	parcel
vowel	empty	silence	prompt
label	empties	absent	tenpence
model	attempt	absence	parent

1 Instead of *p* in <u>pence</u> write: *f, h, sil, abs, lic, def, sci, viol, differ, excell.*

The noun **silence** is formed from the adjective **silent**. Form nouns in the same way from these adjectives:

    2 absent   **3** present   **4** violent   **5** different

Write the plural of the se nouns:

    6 label   **7** towel   **8** rebel   **9** party   **10** country

11 Write these in alphabetical order: **silence, science, defence, duties, difference, promptly, parcel.**

12 Solve this crossword puzzle:

Across

1 A package wrapped in paper.
4 A reason or explanation for something.
5 Cloths with which to dry yourself.

Down

1 Mother or father.
2 These tell what is inside.
3 This breaks, stopping the electricity.

Doctor	Captain	London	McDonald
Major	Sergeant	Belfast	O'Brien
Lord	Corporal	Birmingham	Johnson
Taylor	Reverend	Manchester	Robinson

When we place the names of people in alphabetical order, the titles do not count. We decide the order by the surname. The first names or initials do not count either, unless the surnames are the same. Thus **Eric Jones** will come before **Ronald Jones** because **E** comes before **R**. In the same way, **B. R. McDonald** comes before **B. T. McDonald**, because **R** comes before **T**.

Now place each of these groups in alphabetical order:

1 Miss Davies, Mrs Evans, Mr Morgan, Capt. Jones.
2 E. Johnson, Don Robinson, G. Baker, Tom Hopkinson.
3 Sir James Adams, Lord McDonald, The Rev. E. Taylor, Capt. Cross, Miss Horner, Dr White, Mrs Gilbert.
4 Hunter, Lewis, O'Brien, Hughes, Lodge, Lamb, Hinks.
5 Bishop, Allen, Barber, Knight, Scott, Shaw, Stanley.
6 James Parker, Colin Morris, C. R. Davies, John Thomas, C. T. Derby, Sue Stephenson, N. Patrick, Flora Macdonald.
7 Liverpool, Manchester, London, Belfast, Dublin, York, Dover, Derby, Glasgow, Cardiff, Swansea, Bristol, Bradford.
8 Maj. E. Douglas, Miss B. W. Stewart, Col. A. Wilson, Sergt. Jones, Mrs S. B. Johnson, Mr C. T. M. Smith, Capt. A. Walker, Lord Woolton.

stern	defeat	reply	Germany
modern	desire	apply	applied
govern	defy	hurry	applying
desert	deny	occupy	behaving

Make new words by adding:

1 *-ly* to stern   **3** *-est* to stern   **5** *-ed* to defend
2 *-ment* to govern   **4** *-ing* to govern   **6** *-er* to desert

Read the rule on page 9, and then make new words by adding *-ing* and *-ed* to each of these verbs:

7 desire   **9** inquire   **11** escape   **13** stare
8 behave   **10** invite   **12** chuckle   **14** huddle

Make new words by adding *-ful*, *-less*, *-ing*, *-ed* to each of:

15 use   **16** care   **17** help   **18** taste   **19** doubt

When you add a suffix to a word ending in *y* which has a consonant before it, you must change the *y* into *i*, except before *i*.
Example: *carry—carried—carrying—carrier*; *pray—praying—prayed—prayer*.

Now add *-ing* and *-ed* to each of these verbs:

20 apply   **22** hurry   **24** defy   **26** copy   **28** pray
21 reply   **23** occupy   **25** deny   **27** bury   **29** play

Write the short words ending in *y* from which these come:

30 occupies   **33** supplies   **36** copies   **39** pitiful
31 replied   **34** satisfies   **37** earlier   **40** liveliness
32 tried   **35** cried   **38** prettier   **41** daintiest

said	cried	remarked	bellowed
asked	replied	demanded	thundered
thought	shouted	wondered	inquired
laughed	whispered	answered	chuckled

After each question write the correct answer from below:

1 "Where are you going?" asked Margaret.
2 "May I have another helping?" asked Keith.
3 "Is the water cold?" cried John.
4 "Why are you picking those apples?" thundered the farmer.
5 "Is it far to the station?" inquired the woman.

"It's almost freezing," shouted back George.
"No, it's just round the corner," answered the postman.
"I am sorry, but there is no more left," said his father.
"I am going shopping," replied her mother.
"Your wife asked me to," chuckled Ronald.

For dictation

(*a*) "What is the noun formed from absent?" asked Miss Lake.
(*b*) "It is absence," answered Margaret.
(*c*) "Why have you locked the gate?" inquired the visitor.
(*d*) "If I didn't lock it, the pony would push it open," laughed the farmer.
(*e*) "Which is the largest city in the world?" demanded the teacher.
(*f*) "Tokyo is," replied Andrew.

England	English	vanish	establish
Scotland	Scottish	polish	escape
Wales	Welsh	punish	estimate
Ireland	Irish	perish	especial

Arrange each of these groups in alphabetical order:

1 finish, perish, punish, polish, parish, publish
2 escape, esquire, establish, especial, essay
3 Ireland, Spain, Scotland, Africa, America, India
4 Instead of *van* in <u>van</u>ish write: *pol*, *pun*, *per*, *ban*, *publ*, *par*, *establ*, *Engl*, <u>*Span*</u>, *Ir*, *Corn*, *Scott*.

If we add *-ment* to **punish**, we get **punishment**. Now make new words by adding *-ment* to the following:

5 amuse	7 pave	9 treat	11 engage
6 move	8 base	10 arrange	12 enjoy

Make new words by adding *-ing* and *-ed* to each of these:

13 escape	15 inquire	17 excite	19 confuse	21 graze
14 estimate	16 chuckle	18 refuse	20 excuse	22 damage

Use the suffixes *-ment*, *-less*, *-ful* five times each to make new words from these:

23 wire	26 sense	29 shape	32 spite	35 disgrace
24 move	27 peace	30 cease	33 agree	36 excite
25 pay	28 price	31 grate	34 fright	37 employ

In the early days of flying, a famous airman once found himself surrounded by
thick fog. He could not see anywhere,
and in those days there were no control
towers to guide him to an airfield. Then
suddenly the fog cleared and he saw that

he was over a town. Just at that moment the engine began to splutter.
It had run out of petrol. The pilot steered his machine towards the
open country and then baled out. But the danger was not over. As his
parachute came down, he noticed that the aeroplane was flying round
in circles. If it touched him he would be killed. Luckily, the plane at
last crashed in a field and the airman landed safely on the road.

notice	aeroplane	guide	circle
office	parachute	guess	suddenly
officer	control	guard	luckily
surround	petrol	guilty	guiltily

Read the rule on page 11, and then make adverbs by adding *-ly*
to these adjectives:

1 lucky	3 merry	5 weary	7 hearty	9 sudden
2 guilty	4 happy	6 hasty	8 clumsy	10 steady

Make new words by adding:

11 *-er* to office	13 *-ed* to circle	15 *-ful* to mercy
12 *-ed* to notice	14 *-ful* to beauty	16 *-ness* to clumsy

eager	strive	music	horrid
eagle	arrive	public	stupid
appear	advice	limit	traffic
beneath	police	spirit	visitor

Notice that by adding the suffix *-ness* to an adjective we can make a noun.
Example: *eager—eagerness, clumsy—clumsiness.*
But remember that when the adjective ends in *y*, you must change the *y* into *i* before adding the suffix.

Now make nouns ending in *-ness* from these adjectives:

1 deaf	4 silly	7 sharp	10 lovely
2 lame	5 tired	8 brief	11 ready
3 ugly	6 scarce	9 early	12 gentle

Make adverbs by adding *-ly* to these adjectives:

13 eager	15 public	17 rapid	19 gentle
14 timid	16 stern	18 vivid	20 capable

21 Instead of *pol* in <u>police</u> write: *off, not, adv, pr, tw, just.*

Write each of these groups in alphabetical order:

22 limit, visit, omit, inhabit, admit, credit, habit
23 rabbit, public, stupid, spirit, permit, rapid
24 defeat, retreat, reader, dearest, beaten, beneath
25 spire, strive, stile, slice, service, tribe, twice
26 timid, traffic, horrid, hearing, tearful, terrific

error	whisker	petal	local
terror	whisper	metal	musical
terrible	whistle	medal	terrific
terrify	thistle	mental	castle

Write the words from the box that rhyme with:

1 thistle   **2** metal   **3** terror   **4** pedal   **5** verify

Make adverbs by adding *-ly* to each of these adjectives:

6 local   **7** mental   **8** musical   **9** terrible   **10** horrible

Make new words by adding:

11 *-er* to whistle   **14** *-ed* to horrify   **17** *-ing* to whistle

12 *-er* to whisper   **15** *-ly* to loyal   **18** *-ing* to terrify

13 *-al* to music   **16** *-ness* to easy   **19** *-ty* to loyal

Write these lists in alphabetical order:

20 terror, horror, hollow, hilly, tunic, marrow, music
21 pedal, petal, mental, metal, medal, loyal, local
22 whistle, thistle, whole, often, soften, castle, cattle
23 This crossword puzzle has been solved. With the help of the definitions below, write out the clues.

¹P	E	²D	A	³L
E		I		O
⁴T	U	N	I	C
A		G		A
⁵L	O	Y	A	L

not at all bright and fresh
to do with the place round about
faithful to duty
lever worked by foot
a leaf-like part of a blossom
short coat worn by soldier

Speak roughly to your little boy
    And beat him when he sneezes.
He only does it to annoy
    Because he knows it teases.

I speak severely to my boy.
    I beat him when he sneezes,
For he can thoroughly enjoy
    The pepper when he pleases!

speak	enjoy	pepper	sneeze
please	annoy	bottle	breeze
tease	enjoyable	cunning	roughly
disease	severely	suppose	thoroughly

Notice that when you make the plural of a word like **breeze**, you simply add **-s**: breeze—breezes, disease—diseases. But in fact it sounds as if you had added **-es**. You don't, however, need the *e* because there is already a silent *e* at the end of the word. In the plural this silent *e* is sounded.

Make the plural of these nouns:

1 sneeze	3 house	5 size	7 squeeze	9 crease
2 sense	4 verse	6 craze	8 noise	10 surprise

due	shriek	receive	rescue
value	priest	deceive	handkerchief
argue	grief	conceit	deceitful
avenue	fierce	ceiling	relief

Notice that the ie or ei in the words in the box is sounded like **ee** in **sweet**.

When the sound is like **ee**, you put *i* before *e*, except after *c*, when it is *e* before *i*.

1 Write the following words in two equal lists according to whether they follow the rule or the exception: **yield**, **shield**, **field**, **deceit**, **ceiling**, **chief**, **conceive**, **receive**.

Make new words by adding **-er** to these. (See rule on page 7.)

2 argue	5 receive	8 use	11 believe	14 score
3 rescue	6 deceive	9 rule	12 cure	15 skate
4 value	7 invade	10 tease	13 manage	16 sparkle

Make the comparative and superlative forms of these adjectives. Example: *fiercer, fiercest*.

| 17 fierce | 19 rare | 21 true | 23 sure | 25 thin |
| 18 scarce | 20 late | 22 brave | 24 gentle | 26 big |

Make new words by adding a prefix (**re-**, **un-**, **dis-**) and a suffix (**-ness**, **-ment**, **-er**, **-ful**) to each of these:

| 27 late | 28 sure | 29 agree | 30 believe | 31 respect |

1 `| | | | |s|h|` To make brighter.   (page 38)

2 `| | |p| | | |` To get ready.   (31)

3 `| | |l| | |` The opposite of to lead.   (31)

4 `|e| | | | |` To say again.   (17)

5 `| |o|o| | |` To pick out or select.   (32)

6 `| | | | |u| |` Place of shelter for ships.   (32)

7 `| | |u| | |` Very well known.   (9)

8 `| | | | |u| |` Full of danger.   (33)

9 `|e| | | | | | |` Power-driven flying machine.   (33)

10 `| | | | |e| |` Hole by which smoke escapes.   (13)

11 `| | | |e| | |` Package wrapped in paper.   (34)

12 `|e| | | | |` The opposite of full.   (34)

13 `| | | | | |e|` Ring worn around wrist.   (19)

14 `| | | |e| | |` Army rank just above corporal.   (35)

15 `| |e| | | |` Next after eleventh.   (12)

16 `|e| | |` To resist boldly or openly.   (36)

17 `| | |e| |` The opposite of old-fashioned.   (36)

18 `| | | | |e| |` The plural of stitch.   (26)

19 `| | | | |e| |` Spoke very softly.   (37)

20 `| | | |e|` To get free.   (38)

21 `|e| | | | | |` Possessing beauty.   (10)

22 `| | | | | |` The opposite of innocent.   (39)

23 `| | | | |` The opposite of depart.   (40)

24 `| | | | | |` Vehicles coming and going in street.   (40)

25 `| | | | | |` Fortified building of the past.   (41)

26 `| | | | | | | |` Completely.   (42)

27 `| | | | | |` Road with trees on both sides.   (43)

28 `| | | | | |` Inside top covering of a room.   (43)

Test yourself

(1)

towel	idle	expect	fuel
level	noble	respect	cruel
bushel	uncle	inspect	picture
angel	title	insect	adventure

(2)

death	dozen	extra	fruit
threat	oven	excuse	orange
instead	linen	excellent	apple
dreadful	listen	except	strawberry

(3)

naughty	music	people	petrol
daughter	picnic	honest	engine
certain	pleasant	wicked	machine
entertain	treasure	amusing	factory

For dictation

Margaret thought she was an excellent artist, but her brother was not so certain. One morning she was putting the finishing touches to a picture of a house.

"I am trying to think of a title for my new painting," she informed her brother. "Have you any ideas?"

John looked at the picture very thoroughly. "Why not call it Home?" he replied after a while.

"But why Home?" inquired Margaret.

"Well, there's no place like it," explained her brother.

For extra work

(1)

bullet	vessel	nature	fortune
bonnet	funnel	figure	fortunate
mirror	channel	endure	continue
woollen	barrel	creature	continuation

(2)

mercy	attend	account	complete
fancy	attack	afford	compete
study	address	occur	company
navy	appear	attendance	companion

(3)

neglect	memory	situation	Arithmetic
select	remember	explanation	area
election	intelligent	information	addition
reflection	intention	examination	subtraction

(4)

discuss	equal	divide	religious
discussion	equator	division	marvellous
secret	unusual	decide	delicious
blanket	usually	decision	precious